Quilts with Style

LEISURE ARTS, INC. • Maumelle, Arkansas

PRODUCTION *team*

EDITORIAL STAFF

Senior Product Director: Pam Stebbins
Creative Art Director: Katherine Laughlin
Publications Director: Leah Lampirez
Technical Editor: Mary Sullivan Hutcheson
Editorial Writer: Susan Frantz Wiles
Art Category Manager: Lora Puls
Graphic Artist: Jessica Bramlett
Prepress Technician: Stephanie Johnson
Contributing Photography Stylist: Sondra Daniel
Contributing Photographer: Ken West

BUSINESS STAFF

President and Chief Executive Officer: Fred F. Pruss
Senior Vice President of Operations: Jim Dittrich
Vice President of Retail Sales: Martha Adams
Chief Financial Officer: Tiffany P. Childers
Controller: Teresa Eby
Information Technology Director: Brian Roden
Director of E-Commerce: Mark Hawkins
Manager of E-Commerce: Robert Young

Library of Congress Control Number: 2015939793
ISBN-13/EAN: 978-1-4647-4327-6
UPC: 0-28906-06650-0

Meet Gudrun Erla

When Gudrun Erla discovered her passion for quilting, she had no idea she would one day own Iceland's first online quilt shop—or that she would have a successful pattern company of her own, GE Designs.

Gudrun says, "I grew up in the southwestern part of Iceland called Selfoss. In my early twenties, I took a quilting class at a local sewing store. A few years later I opened the online quilt shop, which grew into two storefront shops. I started designing patterns in Icelandic for use at the store. An American wholesaler asked me to translate the patterns into English to sell in the US."

Soon after that, her husband's career brought the couple and their three children to Minnesota in 2003. She has been designing quilt patterns full time ever since from her home office. Gudrun also began designing fabrics for Red Rooster Fabrics in 2006.

More of her work can be seen at gequiltdesigns.com. To keep up with her busy schedule of quilting classes and other activities, visit her GE Designs page on Facebook.

What's your design style? Bright, active colors? Soft, mellow shades? Pretty prints or stunning solids? These fun-to-make quilts will capture any mood you wish, depending entirely on your fabric selections. Gudrun Erla's patterns include crib and lap quilts as well as bed-size quilts. Each pattern was sewn in a second color family, and charts are provided to change the size of your project—giving you more possibilities for your own exciting quilts!

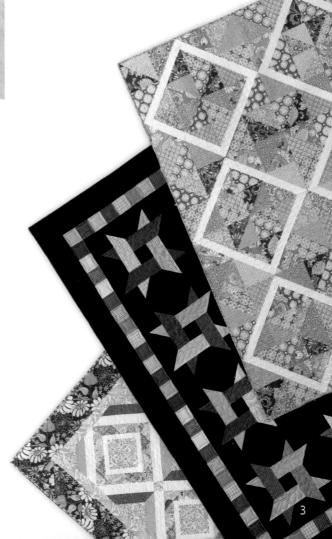

Table of Contents

This lap quilt is fat-quarter friendly and will warm its surroundings with its mostly earthen hues. The narrow cream-colored inner rectangles form a "frame" inside each block, making this layout an excellent way to show off a favorite fabric in the block's center. The second version goes graphic on page 8.

Finished Lap Quilt Size:
61" x 71" (155 cm x 180 cm)
Finished Block Size:
10" x 14" (25 cm x 36 cm)

Pieced by Yvonne Geske
Quilted by Harriet Bollig

simply rectangles TRADITIONAL

FABRIC REQUIREMENTS

Yardage is based on 43"/44" (109 cm/112 cm) wide fabric with a "usable" width of 40" (102 cm). Fat quarters are approximately 21" x 18" (53 cm x 46 cm).

- 15 fat quarters of assorted prints
- 1¼ yds (1.1 m) of cream print
- 4½ yds (4.1 m) of fabric for backing
- ⅝ yd (57 cm) of fabric for binding*

You will also need:

- 69" x 79" (175 cm x 201 cm) piece of batting

*Straight-grain binding for quilt shown was cut from a diagonally striped fabric.

CUTTING THE PIECES

*Follow **Rotary Cutting**, page 53. Cut strips from yardage from the selvage-to-selvage width of the fabric. Cut strips from fat quarters parallel to long edge. Measurements include ¼" seam allowances.*

From *each* fat quarter:

- Cut 1 strip 4½" wide. From this strip, cut 2 **center rectangles** 4½" x 8½".
- Cut 1 strip 10½" wide. From this strip, cut 8 **outer rectangles** 2½" x 10½".

From cream print:

- Cut 25 strips 1½" wide. From these strips, cut 60 **large inner rectangles** 1½" x 8½" and 60 **small inner rectangles** 1½" x 6½".

From fabric for binding:

- Cut 8 **binding strips** 2½" wide.

MAKING THE BLOCKS

*Follow **Piecing**, page 54, and **Pressing**, page 55, to make quilt top. Use ¹/₄" seam allowances throughout.*

1. For Block, select 4 **outer rectangles** from one print, 1 **center rectangle** from a contrasting print, 2 **large inner rectangles**, and 2 **small inner rectangles**.
2. Sew 2 **large inner rectangles** and 1 **center rectangle** together to make **Unit 1**.

Unit 1

3. Sew 2 **small inner rectangles** and **Unit 1** together to make **Unit 2**.

Unit 2

4. Sew 2 **outer rectangles** and **Unit 2** together to make **Unit 3**.

Unit 3

5. Sew 2 **outer rectangles** and **Unit 3** together to make **Block**.
6. Repeat Steps 1-5 to make a total of 30 Blocks.

Block (make 30)

ASSEMBLING THE QUILT TOP

Refer to photo, page 6, to assemble quilt top.

1. Sew 6 **Blocks** together to make **Row**. Make 5 Rows.
2. Sew **Rows** together to complete quilt top.

COMPLETING THE QUILT

1. Follow **Machine Quilting**, page 55, to mark, layer, and quilt as desired. Quilt shown was machine quilted with an all-over flower and leaf pattern.
2. Follow **Making a Hanging Sleeve**, page 57, if a hanging sleeve is desired.
3. Use **binding strips** and follow **Binding**, page 57, to bind quilt.

simply rectangles
MODERN

Let the fabrics fall at random in your Simply Rectangles quilt, and you'll have an amazing collage of color. Gudrun chose a mostly pink, black, and white theme when she made this youthful quilt.

Finished Lap Quilt Size: 61" x 71" (155 cm x 180 cm)
Finished Block Size: 10" x 14" (25 cm x 36 cm)

Pieced by Yvonne Geske • Quilted by Harriet Bollig

The modern version of Simply Rectangles is constructed the same as the traditional version with the following exceptions.

1. A total of 21 black and white print fat quarters, some with pink, lime green, or red, were used.
2. An accent fabric was not used. Instead, each block contains a center rectangle from one print, inner rectangles from a second print, and outer rectangles from a third print.

SIMPLY RECTANGLES OPTIONAL SIZES

	CRIB	TWIN
Finished size	41" x 57" (104 cm x 145 cm)	61" x 85" (155 cm x 216 cm)
Blocks	16 (4 x 4)	36 (6 x 6)

Fabric requirements	8 (traditional)
	   or 12 (modern) assorted print fat quarters
	$3/4$ yd (69 cm) of accent fabric (traditional)
	$3^5/8$ yds (3.3 m) of fabric for backing
	$1/2$ yd (46 cm) of fabric for binding
		18 (traditional)
		   or 26 (modern) assorted print fat quarters
		$1^3/8$ yds (1.3 m) of accent fabric (traditional)
		$5^1/4$ yds (4.8 m) of fabric for backing
		$5/8$ yd (57 cm) of fabric for binding

You will also need	49" x 65" (124 cm x 165 cm) piece of batting	69" x 93" (175 cm x 236 cm) piece of batting
Cut pieces	16 **center rectangles** $4^1/2$" x $8^1/2$" 64 **outer rectangles** $2^1/2$" x $10^1/2$" 32 **large inner rectangles** $1^1/2$" x $8^1/2$" 32 **small inner rectangles** $1^1/2$" x $6^1/2$" 6 **binding strips** $2^1/2$" wide	36 **center rectangles** $4^1/2$" x $8^1/2$" 144 **outer rectangles** $2^1/2$" x $10^1/2$" 72 **large inner rectangles** $1^1/2$" x $8^1/2$" 72 **small inner rectangles** $1^1/2$" x $6^1/2$" 8 **binding strips** $2^1/2$" wide

	FULL	QUEEN	KING
Finished size	81" x 85" (206 cm x 216 cm)	91" x 99"(231 cm x 251 cm)	101" x 99" (257 cm x 251 cm)
Blocks	48 (8 x 6)	63 (9 x 7)	70 (10 x 7)

Fabric requirements	24 (traditional)
	   or 34 (modern) assorted print fat quarters
	$1^7/8$ yds (1.7 m) of accent fabric (traditional)
	$7^1/2$ yds (6.9 m) of fabric for backing
	$3/4$ yd (69 cm) of fabric for binding
		32 (traditional)
		   or 45 (modern) assorted print fat quarters
		$2^1/2$ yds (2.3 m) of accent fabric (traditional)
		$8^1/4$ yds (7.5 m) of fabric for backing
		$7/8$ yd (80 cm) of fabric for binding
			35 (traditional)
			   or 49 (modern) assorted print fat quarters
			$2^3/4$ yds (2.5 m) of accent fabric (traditional)
			9 yds (8.2 m) of fabric for backing
			$7/8$ yd (80 cm) of fabric for binding

You will also need	89" x 93" (226 cm x 236 cm) piece of batting	99" x 107" (251 cm x 272 cm) piece of batting	109" x 107" (277 cm x 272 cm) piece of batting
Cut pieces	48 **center rectangles** $4^1/2$" x $8^1/2$" 192 **outer rectangles** $2^1/2$" x $10^1/2$" 96 **large inner rectangles** $1^1/2$" x $8^1/2$" 96 **small inner rectangles** $1^1/2$" x $6^1/2$" 9 **binding strips** $2^1/2$" wide	63 **center rectangles** $4^1/2$" x $8^1/2$" 252 **outer rectangles** $2^1/2$" x $10^1/2$" 126 **large inner rectangles** $1^1/2$" x $8^1/2$" 126 **small inner rectangles** $1^1/2$" x $6^1/2$" 11 **binding strips** $2^1/2$" wide	70 **center rectangles** $4^1/2$" x $8^1/2$" 280 **outer rectangles** $2^1/2$" x $10^1/2$" 140 **large inner rectangles** $1^1/2$" x $8^1/2$" 140 **small inner rectangles** $1^1/2$" x $6^1/2$" 11 **binding strips** $2^1/2$" wide

So simple, it's elegant—this version of the Homebound quilt uses just two print fabrics on a clean white background. Gudrun also chose white binding to give the quilt an updated look. To see Homebound in a different style, turn to page 15. On page 14, see what you can do with these blocks just by changing direction!

Finished Lap Quilt Size:
49" x 65" (124 cm x 165 cm)
Finished Block Size:
8" x 8" (20 cm x 20 cm)

Pieced by Yvonne Geske
Quilted by Rita Kroening

homebound
MODERN

FABRIC REQUIREMENTS

Yardage is based on 43"/44" (109 cm/112 cm) wide fabric with a "usable" width of 40" (102 cm).
- 1¼ yds (1.1 m) of red print
- 1¼ yds (1.1 m) of blue print
- 1 yd (91 cm) of white print
- 4⅛ yds (3.8 m) of fabric for backing
- ⅝ yd (57 cm) of fabric for binding

You will also need:
- 57" x 73" (145 cm x 185 cm) piece of batting

CUTTING THE PIECES

Follow Rotary Cutting, page 53. Cut strips from the selvage-to-selvage width of the fabric.

From red print:
- Cut 3 strips 6½" wide. Cut these strips in half to make 6 **wide strips**.
- Cut 3 strips 4½" wide. Cut these strips in half to make 6 **medium strips**.
- Cut 3 strips 2½" wide. Cut these strips in half to make 6 **narrow strips**.

From blue print:
- Cut 3 strips 6½" wide. Cut these strips in half to make 6 **wide strips**.
- Cut 3 strips 4½" wide. Cut these strips in half to make 6 **medium strips**.
- Cut 3 strips 2½" wide. Cut these strips in half to make 6 **narrow strips**.

From white print:
- Cut 12 strips 2½" wide. Cut these strips in half to make 24 **narrow strips**.

From fabric for binding:
- Cut 7 **binding strips** 2½" wide.

MAKING THE BLOCKS

Follow Piecing, page 54, and Pressing, page 55, to make quilt top. Use ¹/₄" seam allowances throughout.

1. Sew 1 red **wide strip** and 1 white **narrow strip** together to make **Strip Set A**. Make 6 Strip Set A's. Cut across Strip Set A's at 2¹/₂" intervals to make 48 **Unit 1's**.

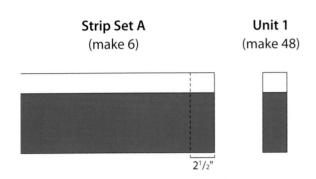

Strip Set A
(make 6)

Unit 1
(make 48)

2¹/₂"

2. Sew 1 red **medium strip**, 1 white **narrow strip**, and 1 blue **narrow strip** together to make **Strip Set B**. Make 6 Strip Set B's. Cut across Strip Set B's at 2¹/₂" intervals to make 48 **Unit 2's**.

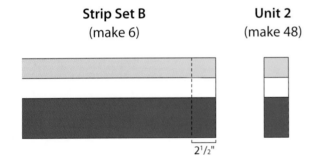

Strip Set B
(make 6)

Unit 2
(make 48)

2¹/₂"

3. Sew 1 red **narrow strip**, 1 white **narrow strip**, and 1 blue **medium strip** together to make **Strip Set C**. Make 6 Strip Set C's. Cut across Strip Set C's at 2¹/₂" intervals to make 48 **Unit 3's**.

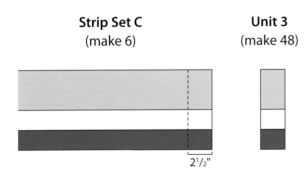

Strip Set C
(make 6)

Unit 3
(make 48)

2¹/₂"

4. Sew 1 white **narrow strip** and 1 blue **wide strip** together to make **Strip Set D**. Make 6 Strip Set D's. Cut across Strip Set D's at 2¹/₂" intervals to make 48 **Unit 4's**.

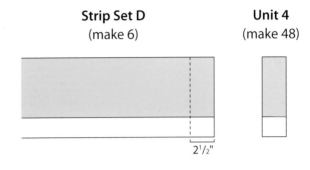

Strip Set D
(make 6)

Unit 4
(make 48)

2¹/₂"

5. Sew 1 **Unit 1**, 1 **Unit 2**, 1 **Unit 3**, and 1 **Unit 4** together to make **Block**. Make 48 Blocks.

Block (make 48)

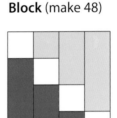

ASSEMBLING THE QUILT TOP CENTER

1. Rotating Blocks as shown, sew 6 **Blocks** together to make **Top Row**. Repeat to make **Bottom Row**.

Top/Bottom Row (make 2)

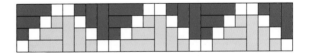

2. Rotating Blocks as shown, sew 6 **Blocks** together to make **Middle Row**. Make 6 Middle Rows.

Middle Row (make 6)

3. Sew **Rows** together to complete quilt top.

13

COMPLETING THE QUILT

1. Follow **Machine Quilting**, page 55, to mark, layer, and quilt as desired. Quilt shown was machine quilted with a continuous swirl pattern.
2. Follow **Making a Hanging Sleeve**, page 57, if a hanging sleeve is desired.
3. Use **binding strips** and follow **Binding**, page 57, to bind quilt.

Quilt Top Diagram

Try rotating your blocks to see what patterns emerge! Shown here are three examples, but you will be able to discover many more options for your own unique quilt!

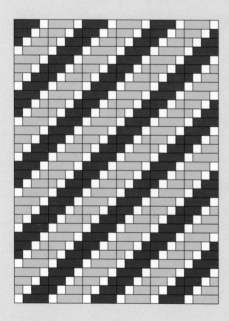

homebound
TRADITIONAL

Looking warmer in a brown theme, Homebound also gains a little shading from the different hues of tan fabric. In the photo below, it's easy to see how the same 8" block gains an alternative look when partially pieced in a third color family.

Finished Lap Quilt Size:
49" x 65" (124 cm x 165 cm)
Finished Block Size:
8" x 8" (20 cm x 20 cm)

Pieced by Yvonne Geske • Quilted by Harriet Bollig

The traditional version of Homebound is constructed the same as the modern version with the these exceptions.

1. This quilt is scrappy. Six tan print fat quarters were used in place of the red print. Three red print and 3 blue print fat quarters were used in place of the blue print. Brown solid was used in place of the white print.
2. The blocks were rotated differently.

HOMEBOUND OPTIONAL SIZES

CRIB		
	Modern	**Traditional**
Finished size	49" x 49" (124 cm x 124 cm)	49" x 49" (124 cm x 124 cm)
Blocks	36 (6 x 6)	36 (6 x 6)
Fabric requirements	1¼ yds (1.1 m) of red print 1¼ yds (1.1 m) of blue print ⅞ yd (80 cm) of white print 3¼ yds (3 m) of fabric for backing ½ yd (46 cm) of fabric for binding	6 tan print fat quarters 3 red print *and* 3 blue print fat quarters 1 yd (91 cm) of brown solid 3¼ yds (3 m) of fabric for backing ½ yd (46 cm) of fabric for binding
You will also need	57" x 57" (145 cm x 145 cm) piece of batting	57" x 57" (145 cm x 145 cm) piece of batting
Cut pieces	5 red and 5 blue **wide strips** 6½" x approx. 20" 5 red and 5 blue **medium strips** 4½" x approx. 20" 5 red, 5 blue, and 20 white **narrow strips** 2½" x approx. 20" 6 **binding strips** 2½" wide	6 tan, 3 red, and 3 blue **wide strips** 6½" x approx. 20" 6 tan, 3 red, and 3 blue **medium strips** 4½" x approx. 20" 6 tan, 3 red, 3 blue, and 24 brown **narrow strips** 2½" x approx. 20" 6 **binding strips** 2½" wide
TWIN		
	Modern	Traditional
Finished size	65" x 81" (165 cm x 206 cm)	65" x 81" (165 cm x 206 cm)
Blocks	80 (8 x 10)	80 (8 x 10)
Fabric requirements	2⅛ yds (1.9 m) of red print 2⅛ yds (1.9 m) of blue print 1⅝ yds (1.5 m) of white print 5 yds (4.6 m) of fabric for backing ⅝ yd (57 cm) of fabric for binding	10 tan print fat quarters 5 red print *and* 5 blue print fat quarters 1⅝ yds (1.5 m) of brown solid 5 yds (4.6 m) of fabric for backing ⅝ yd (57 cm) of fabric for binding
You will also need	73" x 89" (185 cm x 226 cm) piece of batting	73" x 89" (185 cm x 226 cm) piece of batting
Cut pieces	10 red and 10 blue **wide strips** 6½" x approx. 20" 10 red and 10 blue **medium strips** 4½" x approx. 20" 10 red, 10 blue, and 40 white **narrow strips** 2½" x approx. 20" 8 **binding strips** 2½" wide	10 tan, 5 red, and 5 blue **wide strips** 6½" x approx. 20" 10 tan, 5 red, and 5 blue **medium strips** 4½" x approx. 20" 10 tan, 5 red, 5 blue, and 40 brown **narrow strips** 2½" x approx. 20" 8 **binding strips** 2½" wide

HOMEBOUND OPTIONAL SIZES

FULL		
	Modern	**Traditional**
Finished size	81" x 81" (206 cm x 206 cm)	81" x 81" (206 cm x 206 cm)
Blocks	100 (10 x 10)	100 (10 x 10)
Fabric requirements	3 yds (2.7 m) of red print 3 yds (2.7 m) of blue print 2 yds (1.8 m) of white print 7$\frac{1}{2}$ yds (6.9 m) of fabric for backing $\frac{3}{4}$ yd (69 cm) of fabric for binding	14 tan print fat quarters 7 red print *and* 7 blue print fat quarters 2$\frac{1}{4}$ yds (2.1 m) of brown solid 7$\frac{1}{2}$ yds (6.9 m) of fabric for backing $\frac{3}{4}$ yd (69 cm) of fabric for binding
You will also need	89" x 89" (226 cm x 226 cm) piece of batting	89" x 89" (226 cm x 226 cm) piece of batting

Cut pieces	13 red and 13 blue **wide strips**
	    6$\frac{1}{2}$" x approx. 20"
	13 red and 13 blue **medium strips**
	    4$\frac{1}{2}$" x approx. 20"
	13 red, 13 blue, and 52 white **narrow**
	    strips 2$\frac{1}{2}$" x approx. 20"
	9 **binding strips** 2$\frac{1}{2}$" wide
		14 tan, 7 red, and 7 blue **wide strips**
		    6$\frac{1}{2}$" x approx. 20"
		14 tan, 7 red, and 8 blue **medium strips**
		    4$\frac{1}{2}$" x approx. 20"
		14 tan, 7 red, 7 blue, and 56 brown
		    narrow strips 2$\frac{1}{2}$" x approx. 20"
		9 **binding strips** 2$\frac{1}{2}$" wide

QUEEN/KING		
	Modern	**Traditional**
Finished size	97" x 97" (246 cm x 246 cm)	97" x 97" (246 cm x 246 cm)
Blocks	144 (12 x 12)	144 (12 x 12)
Fabric requirements	3$\frac{3}{4}$ yds (3.4 m) of red print 3$\frac{3}{4}$ yds (3.4 m) of blue print 2$\frac{3}{4}$ yds (2.5 m) of white print 8$\frac{3}{4}$ yds (8 m) of fabric for backing $\frac{7}{8}$ yd (80 cm) of fabric for binding	18 tan print fat quarters 9 red print *and* 9 blue print fat quarters 2$\frac{3}{4}$ yds (2.5 m) of brown solid 8$\frac{3}{4}$ yds (8 m) of fabric for backing $\frac{7}{8}$ yd (80 cm) of fabric for binding
You will also need	105" x 105" (267 cm x 267 cm) piece of batting	105" x 105" (267 cm x 267 cm) piece of batting

Cut pieces	18 red and 18 blue **wide strips**
	    6$\frac{1}{2}$" x approx. 20"
	18 red and 18 blue **medium strips**
	    4$\frac{1}{2}$" x approx. 20"
	18 red, 18 blue, and 72 white **narrow**
	    strips 2$\frac{1}{2}$" x approx. 20"
	11 **binding strips** 2$\frac{1}{2}$" wide
		18 tan, 9 red, and 9 blue **wide strips**
		    6$\frac{1}{2}$" x approx. 20"
		18 tan, 9 red, and 9 blue **medium strips**
		    4$\frac{1}{2}$" x approx. 20"
		18 tan, 9 red, 9 blue, and 72 brown
		    narrow strips 2$\frac{1}{2}$" x approx. 20"
		11 **binding strips** 2$\frac{1}{2}$" wide

Gudrun designed this large lap quilt so that the colorful designs are floating on the cream background. It's a clever way to avoid losing the points in the seams when joining the blocks together. Cozy flannel adds a little warmth to the second version, shown on page 23.

Finished Lap Quilt Size
63" x 75" (160 cm x 191 cm)
Finished Block Size
12" x 12" (30 cm x 30 cm)

Pieced by Gudrun Erl
Quilted by Rita Kroening

sand dollars
MODERN

FABRIC REQUIREMENTS

Yardage is based on 43"/44" (109 cm/112 cm) wide fabric with a "usable" width of 40" (102 cm). Jelly roll strips are 2¹/₂" x approximately 40" (6 cm x 102 cm). Fat quarters are approximately 21" x 18" (53 cm x 46 cm).

- 20 jelly roll strips (5 *each* of 4 color groups: blue, green, red/peach, and yellow/brown) (8 fat quarters [2 of each color group] may be used instead, but will provide less variety)
- 2³/₄ yds (2.5 m) of cream solid
- 1⁵/₈ yds (1.5 m) of blue floral
- 4⁵/₈ yds (4.2 m) of fabric for backing
- ⁵/₈ yd (57 cm) of fabric for binding

You will also need:
- 71" x 83" (180 cm x 211 cm) piece of batting

CUTTING THE PIECES

*Follow **Rotary Cutting**, page 53. Cut strips from yardage from the selvage-to-selvage width of the fabric. Cut strips from fat quarters parallel to long edge. Measurements include ¹/₄" seam allowances.*

From *each* color group of jelly roll strips *or* fat quarters:
- Cut 20 sets of 1 **square** 2¹/₂" x 2¹/₂" and 1 **rectangle** 2¹/₂" x 6¹/₂". (Each set should be cut from 1 fabric.)

From cream solid:
- Cut 8 strips 3¹/₂" wide. From these strips, cut 80 **large background squares** 3¹/₂" x 3¹/₂".
- Cut 2 strips 2¹/₂" wide. From these strips, cut 20 **small background squares** 2¹/₂" x 2¹/₂".
- Cut 10 strips 3¹/₂" wide. From these strips, cut 80 **large background rectangles** 3¹/₂" x 4¹/₂".
- Cut 8 strips 2¹/₂" wide. From these strips, cut 80 **small background rectangles** 2¹/₂" x 3¹/₂".

From blue floral:
- Cut 7 **border strips** 7¹/₂" wide.

From fabric for binding:
- Cut 8 **binding strips** 2¹/₂" wide.

MAKING THE BLOCKS

*Follow **Piecing**, page 54, and **Pressing**, page 55, to make quilt top. Use ¼" seam allowances throughout.*

1. For **Block**, select 1 set of 1 **square** and 1 **rectangle** from *each* of the 4 color groups. You will also need 4 **large background squares**, 1 **small background square**, 4 **large background rectangles**, and 4 **small background rectangles**.

2. Draw a diagonal line (corner to corner) on wrong side of each **square**.

3. With right sides together, place 1 **square** on 1 **large background rectangle** as shown *(Fig. 1)*. Stitch along drawn line. Trim ¼" from stitching line *(Fig. 2)*. Open up and press seam allowances toward triangle to make **Unit 1**. Make 4 Unit 1's, 1 from each color group.

Fig. 1

Fig. 2

Unit 1 (make 4)

4. Sew 1 **large background square** and 1 **Unit 1** together to make **Unit 2**. Make 4 Unit 2's.

Unit 2 (make 4)

5. With right sides together, place 1 **small background rectangle** on 1 **rectangle** as shown *(Fig. 3)*. Stitch diagonally. Trim ¼" from stitching line *(Fig. 4)*. Open up and press to make **Unit 3**. Make 4 Unit 3's.

Fig. 3   **Fig. 4**

Unit 3 (make 4)

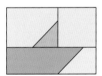

6. Referring to **Block** diagram, page 22, arrange 4 Unit 2's, 4 Unit 3's and 1 **small background square** on a flat surface.

7. Sew 1 **Unit 2** and 1 **Unit 3** together to make **Unit 4**. Make 4 Unit 4's.

Unit 4 (make 4)

8. Using a "partial seam," sew **small background square** to 1 **Unit 4** as shown, stopping halfway across small background square *(Fig. 5)*.

Fig. 5

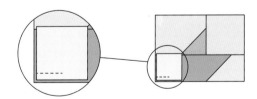

9. Sew a second Unit 4 to left side of small background square. Sew a third and fourth Unit 4 to small background square *(Fig. 6)*.

Fig. 6

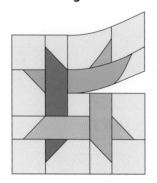

10. Finish sewing the partial seam of the first Unit 4 to complete **Block**.
11. Repeat Steps 1-10 to make a total of 20 Blocks.

Block (make 20)

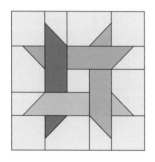

ASSEMBLING THE QUILT TOP CENTER

*Refer to **Quilt Top Diagram** to assemble quilt top.*
1. Sew 4 **Blocks** together make **Row**. Make 5 Rows.
2. Sew **Rows** together to complete quilt top.

ADDING THE BORDER

1. Sew **border strips** together end to end to make one continuous strip.
2. To determine length of **side borders**, measure *length* across center of quilt top center. Cut 2 side borders from continuous strip. Matching centers and corners, sew side borders to quilt top center.

3. To determine length of **top/bottom borders**, measure *width* across center of quilt top center (including added borders). Cut 2 top/bottom borders from continuous strip. Matching centers and corners, sew top/bottom borders to quilt top center.

COMPLETING THE QUILT

1. Follow **Machine Quilting**, page 55, to mark, layer, and quilt as desired. Quilt shown was machine quilted. Feather patterns were quilted in the border and the color print portions of the blocks. The background centers of the blocks were quilted with a curved square and the remainder of the background was meander quilted.
2. Follow **Making a Hanging Sleeve**, page 57, if a hanging sleeve is desired.
3. Use **binding strips** and follow **Binding**, page 57, to bind quilt.

Quilt Top Diagram

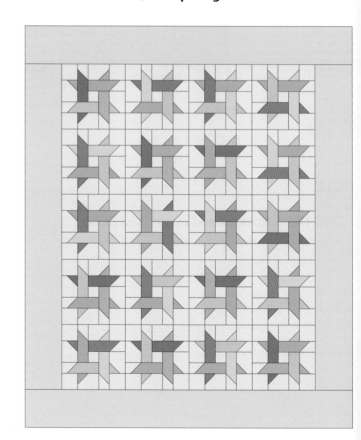

flannel makes this darker version of Sand Dollars so inviting to the touch! The ize is perfect for a crib quilt r a large wall hanging.

Finished Crib Quilt Size: 47" x 59" (119 cm x 150 cm)
Finished Block Size: 12" x 12" (30 cm x 30 cm)

Pieced by Gudrun Erla and Yvonne Geske
Quilted by Rita Kroening

The smaller traditional version of Sand Dollars is constructed the same as the traditional version with the following exceptions.

1. Flannel fabric was used. The background is a black/brown check flannel.
2. There are only 12 blocks. An inner pieced border was added using 88 border squares 2½" x 2½" (cut size). The outer border, cut from the black/brown check flannel, is 3½" wide (cut size). See charts, pages 24-25, for more information.

SAND DOLLARS OPTIONAL SIZES

	CRIB	TWIN
Finished size	47" x 59" (119 cm x 150 cm)	63" x 87" (160 cm x 221 cm)
Blocks	12 (3 x 4)	24 (4 x 6)
Fabric requirements	3 jelly roll strips *or* 1 fat quarter *each* of 4 color groups (modern)* *or* 5 jelly roll strips *or* 2 fat quarters *each* of 4 color groups (traditional)* 1³/₄ yds (1.6 m) (modern) *or* 2³/₈ yds (2.2 m) (traditional) of background fabric 1¹/₈ yds (1 m) of fabric for border (modern) 3³/₄ yds (3.4 m) of fabric for backing ¹/₂ yd (46 cm) of fabric for binding *Fat quarters will provide less variety.	6 jelly roll strips *or* 2 fat quarters *each* of 4 color groups (modern)* *or* 8 jelly roll strips *or* 3 fat quarters *each* of 4 color groups (traditional)* 3¹/₈ yds (2.9 m) (modern) *or* 4¹/₂ yds (4.1 m) (traditional) of background fabric 1⁷/₈ yds (1.7 m) of fabric for border (modern) 5³/₈ yds (4.9 m) of fabric for backing ³/₄ yd (69 cm) of fabric for binding *Fat quarters will provide less variety.
You will also need	55" x 67" (140 cm x 170 cm) piece of batting	71" x 95" (180 cm x 241 cm) piece of batting
Cut pieces	48 sets of 1 **square** 2¹/₂" x 2¹/₂" and 1 **rectangle** 2¹/₂" x 6¹/₂" (12 sets from *each* color group) 88 **border squares** 2¹/₂" x 2¹/₂" (traditional) 48 **large background squares** 3¹/₂" x 3¹/₂" 12 **small background squares** 2¹/₂" x 2¹/₂" 48 **large background rectangles** 3¹/₂" x 4¹/₂" 48 **small background rectangles** 2¹/₂" x 3¹/₂" 6 **border strips** 5¹/₂" wide (modern) *or* 6 **border strips** 3¹/₂" wide (traditional) 6 **binding strips** 2¹/₂" wide	96 sets of 1 **square** 2¹/₂" x 2¹/₂" and 1 **rectangle** 2¹/₂" x 6¹/₂" (24 sets from *each* color group) 124 **border squares** 2¹/₂" x 2¹/₂" (traditional) 96 **large background squares** 3¹/₂" x 3¹/₂" 24 **small background squares** 2¹/₂" x 2¹/₂" 96 **large background rectangles** 3¹/₂" x 4¹/₂" 96 **small background rectangles** 2¹/₂" x 3¹/₂" 8 **border strips** 7¹/₂" wide (modern) *or* 8 **border strips** 5¹/₂" wide (traditional) 9 **binding strips** 2¹/₂" wide

SAND DOLLARS OPTIONAL SIZES

	FULL	QUEEN	KING
Finished size	75" x 87" (191 cm x 221 cm)	87" x 99" (221 cm x 251 cm)	99" x 99" (251 cm x 251 cm)
Blocks	30 (5 x 6)	42 (6 x 7)	49 (7 x 7)
Fabric requirements	8 jelly roll strips *or* 3 fat quarters *each* of 4 color groups (modern)* *or* 11 jelly roll strips *or* 4 fat quarters *each* of 4 color groups (traditional)* $3^{7}/_{8}$ yds (3.5 m) (modern) *or* $5^{1}/_{8}$ yds (4.7 m) (traditional) of background fabric $1^{7}/_{8}$ yds (1.7 m) of fabric for border (modern) 7 yds (6.4 m) of fabric for backing $^{3}/_{4}$ yd (69 cm) of fabric for binding *Fat quarters will provide less variety.	11 jelly roll strips *or* 3 fat quarters *each* of 4 color groups (modern)* *or* 14 jelly roll strips *or* 4 fat quarters *each* of 4 color groups (traditional)* $5^{1}/_{2}$ yds (5 m) (modern) *or* $7^{1}/_{8}$ yds (6.5 m) (traditional) of background fabric $2^{3}/_{8}$ yds (2.2 m) of fabric for border (modern) 8 yds (7.3 m) of fabric for backing $^{7}/_{8}$ yd (80 cm) of fabric for binding *Fat quarters will provide less variety.	13 jelly roll strips *or* 4 fat quarters *each* of 4 color groups (modern)* *or* 16 jelly roll strips *or* 5 fat quarters *each* of 4 color groups (traditional)* $6^{3}/_{8}$ yds (5.8 m) (modern) *or* 8 yds (7.3 m) (traditional) of background fabric $2^{3}/_{8}$ yds (2.2 m) of fabric for border (modern) 9 yds (8.2 m) of fabric for backing $^{7}/_{8}$ yd (80 cm) of fabric for binding *Fat quarters will provide less variety.
You will also need	83" x 95" (211 cm x 241 cm) piece of batting	95" x 107" (241 cm x 272 cm) piece of batting	107" x 107" (272 cm x 272 cm) piece of batting
Cut pieces	120 sets of 1 **square** $2^{1}/_{2}$" x $2^{1}/_{2}$" and 1 **rectangle** $2^{1}/_{2}$" x $6^{1}/_{2}$" (30 sets from *each* color group) 136 **borders squares** $2^{1}/_{2}$" x $2^{1}/_{2}$" (traditional) 120 **large background squares** $3^{1}/_{2}$" x $3^{1}/_{2}$" 30 **small background squares** $2^{1}/_{2}$" x $2^{1}/_{2}$" 120 **large background rectangles** $3^{1}/_{2}$" x $4^{1}/_{2}$" 120 **small background rectangles** $2^{1}/_{2}$" x $3^{1}/_{2}$" 8 **border strips** $7^{1}/_{2}$" wide (modern) *or* 8 **border strips** $5^{1}/_{2}$" wide (traditional) 9 **binding strips** $2^{1}/_{2}$" wide	168 sets of 1 **square** $2^{1}/_{2}$" x $2^{1}/_{2}$" and 1 **rectangle** $2^{1}/_{2}$" x $6^{1}/_{2}$ (42 sets from *each* color group) 160 **borders squares** $2^{1}/_{2}$" x $2^{1}/_{2}$" (traditional) 168 **large background squares** $3^{1}/_{2}$" x $3^{1}/_{2}$" 42 **small background squares** $2^{1}/_{2}$" x $2^{1}/_{2}$" 168 **large background rectangles** $3^{1}/_{2}$" x $4^{1}/_{2}$" 168 **small background rectangles** $2^{1}/_{2}$" x $3^{1}/_{2}$" 10 **border strips** $7^{1}/_{2}$" wide (modern) *or* 10 **border strips** $5^{1}/_{2}$" wide (traditional) 11 **binding strips** $2^{1}/_{2}$" wide	196 sets of 1 **square** $2^{1}/_{2}$" x $2^{1}/_{2}$" and 1 **rectangle** $2^{1}/_{2}$" x $6^{1}/_{2}$" (49 sets from *each* color group) 172 **borders squares** $2^{1}/_{2}$" x $2^{1}/_{2}$" (traditional) 196 **large background squares** $3^{1}/_{2}$" x $3^{1}/_{2}$" 49 **small background squares** $2^{1}/_{2}$" x $2^{1}/_{2}$" 196 **large background rectangles** $3^{1}/_{2}$" x $4^{1}/_{2}$" 196 **small background rectangles** $2^{1}/_{2}$" x $3^{1}/_{2}$" 10 **border strips** $7^{1}/_{2}$" wide (modern) *or* 10 **border strips** $5^{1}/_{2}$" wide (traditional) 11 **binding strips** $2^{1}/_{2}$" wide

Riptide is created from a versatile block that may very well become your favorite! Each block is cut from a three-color strip set and has triangles added in two opposing corners. Even the cut-away corners aren't wasted when you use them to make the bonus Riptide Table Runner on page 32. Just for fun, try arranging a few of your main blocks in different configurations before you sew them into this Riptide quilt. You may be surprised at the familiar patterns you'll discover. Just a few possibilities are shown on page 31. If you like quilts with a touch of black, check out the second version on page 33.

Finished Crib/Lap Quilt Size:
49" x 61" (124 cm x 155 cm)
Finished Block Size:
6" x 6" (15 cm x 15 cm)

Pieced by Gudrun Erla
Quilted by Rita Kroening

riptide
TRADITIONAL

FABRIC REQUIREMENTS

Yardage is based on 43"/44" (109 cm/112 cm) wide fabric with a "usable" width of 40" (102 cm). Jelly roll strips are 2¹/₂" x approximately 40" (6 cm x 102 cm). Fat quarters are approximately 21" x 18" (53 cm x 46 cm).

- 42 jelly roll strips of assorted prints (red, orange, brown, aqua, and pink) (12 fat quarters may be used instead, but will provide less variety)
- 1⁵/₈ yds (1.5 m) of cream print
- 3⁷/₈ yds (3.5 m) of fabric for backing
- ¹/₂ yd (46 cm) of fabric for binding

You will also need:
- 57" x 69" (145 cm x 175 cm) piece of batting

CUTTING THE PIECES

*Follow **Rotary Cutting**, page 53. Cut strips from yardage from the selvage-to-selvage width of the fabric. Cut strips from fat quarters parallel to long edge. Do not cut jelly roll strips. Measurements include ¹/₄" seam allowances.*

From assorted print fat quarters:
- Cut a total of 81 **strips** 2¹/₂" wide.

From cream print:
- Cut 15 strips 3¹/₂" wide. From these strips, cut 160 **squares** 3¹/₂" x 3¹/₂".

From fabric for binding:
- Cut 6 **binding strips** 2¹/₂" wide.

MAKING THE BLOCKS

*Follow **Piecing**, page 54, and **Pressing**, page 55, to make quilt top. Use 1/4" seam allowances throughout.*

1. Sew 3 assorted jelly roll strips *or* 3 assorted **strips** cut from fat quarters together to make **Strip Set**. Make 14 Strip Sets from jelly roll strips *or* 27 Strip Sets from fat quarter strips. Cut across Strip Sets at 6 1/2" intervals to make 80 **Unit 1's**.

Strip Set (make 14 *or* 27)

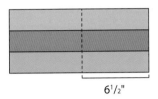

6 1/2"

Unit 1 (make 80)

2. Draw diagonal line (corner to corner) on wrong side of 1 cream print **square**. Draw a second line 1/2" from first line *(Fig. 1)*. Repeat for remaining cream print squares.

Fig. 1

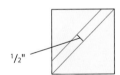

1/2"

3. With right sides together, place 1 square on opposite corners of 1 Unit 1 as shown and stitch along drawn lines *(Fig. 2)*. Repeat with remaining squares and Unit 1's.

Fig. 2

4. Cut halfway between stitched lines *(Fig. 3)* and press open to make 1 **Block** and 2 **Triangle-Squares**. Make 80 Blocks and 160 Triangle-Squares. Set Triangle-Squares aside for bonus table runner, page 32.

Fig. 3

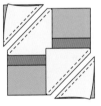

Block (make 80)

Triangle-Square (make 160)

ASSEMBLING THE QUILT TOP

1. Rotating every other Block 90°, sew 8 **Blocks** together to make **Row**. Make 10 Rows.

Row (make 10)

2. Referring to **Quilt Top Diagram** and rotating every other Row, sew **Rows** together to complete quilt top.

COMPLETING THE QUILT

1. Follow **Machine Quilting**, page 55, to mark, layer, and quilt as desired. Quilt shown was machine quilted. A flower design was quilted in each cream area, and a feather design was quilted in the remainder of the quilt.
2. Follow **Making a Hanging Sleeve**, page 57, if a hanging sleeve is desired.
3. Use **binding strips** and follow **Binding**, page 57, to bind quilt.

Quilt Top Diagram

It is surprising how many different patterns can be formed by simply rotating these simple blocks! Using these diagrams as suggestions, experiment with your own blocks on a design wall or empty floor space.

riptide
TABLE RUNNER

Finished Table Runner Size: 17" x 41"
(43 cm x 104 cm)
Finished Block Size: 4" x 4" (10 cm x 10 cm)

This table runner is made using the set-aside Triangle-Squares from the Riptide quilt, page 26.

ADDITIONAL FABRIC REQUIREMENTS

$1^3/_8$ yds (1.3 m) of fabric for backing
$^3/_8$ yd (34 cm) of fabric for binding*
You will also need:
25" x 49" (64 cm x 124 cm) piece of batting

*Straight grain-binding for table runner shown was cut from a diagonally striped fabric.

MAKING THE TABLE RUNNER

1. Trim each **Triangle-Square** to $2^1/_2$" x $2^1/_2$", cutting off as much of the small triangle along the seamline as possible *(Fig. 1)*.

Fig. 1

2. Sew 4 Triangle-Squares together to make **Block**. Make 40 Blocks.

Block (make 40)

3. Referring to **Table Runner Diagram**, sew 4 **Blocks** together to make **Row**. Make 10 Rows.
4. Sew **Rows** together to make table runner top.
5. Follow **Machine Quilting**, page 55, to mark, layer, and quilt as desired.
6. Cut 4 **binding strips** $2^1/_2$" wide and follow **Binding**, page 57, to bind table runner.

Table Runner Diagram

The turn of a block can make all the difference! The colorful zigzags on this lap-size version of the Riptide quilt are eye-catching against the black background. This lap quilt is perfect for a child's room.

Finished Crib/Lap Quilt Size: 54" x 66" (137 cm x 168 cm)
Finished Block Size: 6" x 6" (15 cm x 15 cm)

Pieced by Yvonne Geske • Quilted by Rita Kroening

The modern version of Riptide is constructed the same as the traditional version with the following exceptions.

1. Instead of a cream print, a black print was used.
2. The blocks were rotated to create a zigzag pattern.
3. A black print border was added. For border, you will need an additional $3/4$ yd (69 cm) of fabric. Cut 7 strips 3" wide. Piecing as necessary, cut 2 **side borders** 3 x $60^1/2$" and 2 **top/bottom borders** 3" x $53^1/2$".
4. You will need $4^1/8$ yds (3.8 m) of fabric for backing and $5/8$ yd (57 cm) of fabric for binding. You will also need a 62" x 74" (157 cm x 188 cm) piece of batting.

RIPTIDE OPTIONAL SIZES

TWIN		
	Traditional	**Modern**
Finished size	61" x 85" (155 cm x 216 cm)	66" x 90" (168 cm x 229 cm)
Blocks	140 (10 x 14)	140 (10 x 14)
Fabric requirements	72 jelly roll strips of assorted prints (21 fat quarters may be used, but will provide less variety) 2⁷/₈ yds (2.6 m) of cream print 5¹/₄ yds (4.8 m) of fabric for backing ⁵/₈ yd (57 cm) of fabric for binding	72 jelly roll strips of assorted prints (21 fat quarters may be used, but will provide less variety) 3⁵/₈ yds (3.3 m) of black print 5¹/₂ yds (5 m) of fabric for backing ³/₄ yd (69 cm) of fabric for binding
You will also need	69" x 93" (175 cm x 236 cm) piece of batting	74" x 98" (188 cm x 249 cm) piece of batting
Cut pieces	141 **strips** 2¹/₂" wide if using fat quarters (do not cut jelly roll strips) 280 **squares** 3¹/₂" x 3¹/₂" 8 **binding strips** 2¹/₂" wide	141 **strips** 2¹/₂" wide if using fat quarters (do not cut jelly roll strips) 280 **squares** 3¹/₂" x 3¹/₂" 9 **border strips** 3" wide 9 **binding strips** 2¹/₂" wide
FULL		
	Traditional	**Modern**
Finished size	73" x 85" (185 cm x 216 cm)	78" x 90" (198 cm x 229 cm)
Blocks	168 (12 x 14)	168 (12 x 14)
Fabric requirements	84 jelly roll strips of assorted prints (24 fat quarters may be used instead, but will provide less variety) 3³/₈ yds (3.1 m) of cream print 6³/₄ yds (6.2 m) of fabric for backing ³/₄ yd (69 cm) of fabric for binding	84 jelly roll strips of assorted prints (24 fat quarters may be used instead, but will provide less variety) 4¹/₄ yds (3.9 m) of black print 7¹/₄ yds (6.6 m) of fabric for backing ⁷/₈ yd (80 cm) of fabric for binding
You will also need	81" x 93" (206 cm x 236 cm) piece of batting	86" x 98" (218 cm x 249 cm) piece of batting
Cut pieces	168 **strips** 2¹/₂" wide if using fat quarters (do not cut jelly roll strips) 336 **squares** 3¹/₂" x 3¹/₂" 9 **binding strips** 2¹/₂" wide	168 **strips** 2¹/₂" wide if using fat quarters (do not cut jelly roll strips) 336 **squares** 3¹/₂" x 3¹/₂" 9 **border strips** 3" wide 10 **binding strips** 2¹/₂" wide

RIPTIDE OPTIONAL SIZES

QUEEN		
	Traditional	**Modern**
Finished size	85" x 97" (216 cm x 246 cm)	90" x 102" (229 cm x 259 ~~cm~~)
Blocks	224 (14 x 16)	224 (14 x 16)
Fabric requirements	114 jelly roll strips of assorted prints (33 fat quarters may be used, but will provide less variety) $4^1/_2$ yds (4.1 m) of cream print $7^3/_4$ yds (7.1 m) of fabric for backing $^7/_8$ yd (80 cm) of fabric for binding	114 jelly roll strip~~s~~ (33 fat qua~~rters~~ ~~will~~ provide ~~less variety~~ $5^1/_2$ yd~~s~~ $8^1/$ ~~for backing~~ ~~fabric for binding~~
You will also need	93" x 105" (236 cm x 267 cm) piece of batting	98" ~~x~~ ~~cm x 279 cm) piece of~~ batti~~ng~~
Cut pieces	225 **strips** $2^1/_2$" wide if using fat quarters (do not cut jelly roll strips) 448 **squares** $3^1/_2$" x $3^1/_2$" 10 **binding strips** $2^1/_2$" wide	225 **strips** $2^1/_2$" wide if using fat quarters (do not cut jelly roll strips) 448 **squares** $3^1/_2$" x $3^1/_2$" 11 **border strips** 3" wide 11 **binding strips** $2^1/_2$" wide
KING		
	Traditional	**Modern**
Finished size	97" x 97" (246 cm x 246 cm)	102" x 102" (259 cm x 259 cm)
Blocks	256 (16 x 16)	256 (16 x 16)
Fabric requirements	129 jelly roll strips of assorted prints (37 fat quarters may be used instead, but will provide less variety) $5^1/_8$ yds (4.7 m) of cream print $8^3/_4$ yds (8 m) of fabric for backing $^7/_8$ yd (80 cm) of fabric for binding	129 jelly roll strips of assorted prints (37 fat quarters may be used instead, but will provide less variety) $6^1/_8$ yds (5.6 m) of black print $9^1/_4$ yds (8.5 m) of fabric for backing 1 yd (91 cm) of fabric for binding
You will also need	105" x 105" (267 cm x 267 cm) piece of batting	110" x 110" (279 cm x 279 cm) piece of batting
Cut pieces	258 **strips** $2^1/_2$" wide if using fat quarters (do not cut jelly roll strips) 512 **squares** $3^1/_2$" x $3^1/_2$" 11 **binding strips** $2^1/_2$" wide	258 **strips** $2^1/_2$" wide if using fat quarters (do not cut jelly roll strips) 512 **squares** $3^1/_2$" x $3^1/_2$" 11 **border strips** 3" wide 12 **binding strips** $2^1/_2$" wide

For the colorful triangles in this generously sized bed quilt, you can use yardage or precut layer cake (10") squares. The blocks are large at 16", and each has a strip of cream running through its middle. When four blocks are sewn together, the cream diamonds are formed. For a dramatic change, the Memory Lane quilt on page 41 uses black fabric strips instead of cream.

Finished Queen/King Quilt Size
97" x 97" (246 cm x 246 cm

Finished Block Size
16" x 16" (41 cm x 41 cm

Pieced by Gudrun Erl
Quilted by Rita Kroenin

memory lane
MODERN

FABRIC REQUIREMENTS

Yardage is based on 43"/44" (109 cm/112 cm) wide fabric with a "usable" width of 40" (102 cm). Layer cake squares are 10" x 10" (25 cm x 25 cm).

- 144 layer cake squares of assorted prints ($^3/_8$ yd [34 cm] *each* of 36 assorted prints may be used instead, but will provide less variety)
- $2^3/_8$ yds (2.2 m) of cream solid fabric
- $8^3/_4$ yds (8 m) of fabric for backing
- $^7/_8$ yd (80 cm) of fabric for binding

You will also need:

- 105" x 105" (267 cm x 267 cm) piece of batting
- $16^1/_2$" or larger square acrylic ruler

CUTTING THE PIECES

*Follow **Rotary Cutting**, page 53. Cut strips from the selvage-to-selvage width of the fabric. Measurements include $^1/_4$" seam allowances.*

From layer cake squares or yardage of assorted prints:
- Cut 144 **squares** $9^1/_2$" x $9^1/_2$".

From cream solid:
- Cut 3 strips 25" wide. From these strips, cut 36 **strips** 25" x $2^1/_2$".

From fabric for binding:
- Cut 11 **binding strips** $2^1/_2$" wide.

MAKING THE BLOCKS

*Follow **Piecing**, page 54, and **Pressing**, page 55, to make quilt top. Use ¹/₄" seam allowances throughout.*

1. Sew 2 **squares** together to make **Unit 1**. Make 2 Unit 1's, pressing in the directions indicated by arrows.

Unit 1 (make 2)

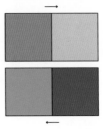

Sew 2 **Unit 1's** together to make **Four Patch**. Before pressing, use a seam ripper to remove the stitches that are in the seam allowances of the seam just made *(Fig. 1)*. Press seam allowances at the intersection open and the remainder of seam allowances in a circular pattern *(Fig. 2)*.

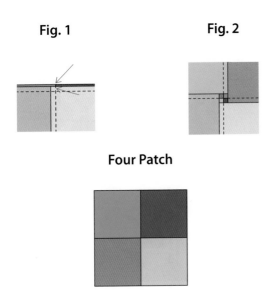

Fig. 1   **Fig. 2**

Four Patch

Using ruler and rotary cutter, cut *twice* diagonally across Four Patch *(Fig. 3)* to make 4 **pieced triangles**.

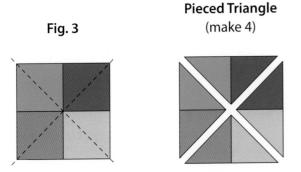

Fig. 3

Pieced Triangle (make 4)

Sew 2 opposite **pieced triangles** together to make **Unit 2**. Make 2 Unit 2's.

Unit 2 (make 2)

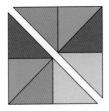

5. Repeat Steps 1-4 to make a total of 72 Unit 2's.
6. Sew 2 **Unit 2's** and 1 **strip** together to make **Unit 3**. Press seam allowances toward strip. Make 36 Unit 3's.

Unit 3 (make 36)

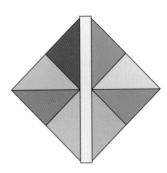

7. Place square ruler on top of 1 Unit 3, aligning outer edge of 16$\frac{1}{2}$" ruler or 16$\frac{1}{2}$" marks of larger ruler with edge of cream strip and 45° angle mark on ruler with seam between 2 pieced triangles *(Fig. 4)*. Trim 2 edges if needed (shown on right side). If using 16$\frac{1}{2}$" ruler, trim remaining 2 sides. If using larger ruler, rotate ruler 180°, aligning 16$\frac{1}{2}$" marks with trimmed edges. Trim remaining 2 edges to make **Block**. Make 36 Blocks.

Fig. 4

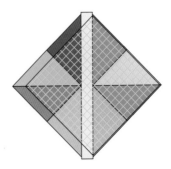

Block (make 36)

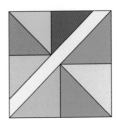

ASSEMBLING THE QUILT TOP

1. Arrange **Blocks** into 6 **Rows** of 6 Blocks each, making sure the cream strips are angled correctly.
2. Sew Blocks together to make Rows.
3. Sew Rows together to complete quilt top.

COMPLETING THE QUILT

1. Follow **Machine Quilting**, page 55, to mark, layer, and quilt as desired. Quilt shown was machine quilted. A swirl pattern was quilted along the cream diamonds, with a larger swirl pattern quilted in the remainder of the quilt.
2. Follow **Making a Hanging Sleeve**, page 57, if a hanging sleeve is desired.
3. Use **binding strips** and follow **Binding**, page 57, to bind quilt.

Quilt Top Diagram

MEMORY LANE OPTIONAL SIZES

	LAP	TWIN
Finished size	65" x 65" (165 cm x 165 cm)	65" x 97" (165 cm x 246 cm)
Blocks	16 (4 x 4)	24 (4 x 6)
Fabric requirements	64 layer cake squares (³/₈ yd [30 cm] *each* of 16 prints may be used instead but will provide less variety) ⁷/₈ yd (80 cm) of contrasting print or solid for strips to make diamond shapes 4¹/₈ yds (3.8 m) of fabric for backing ⁵/₈ yd (57 cm) of fabric for binding	96 layer cake squares (³/₈ yd [30 cm] *each* of 24 prints may be used instead but will provide less variety) 1⁵/₈ yds (1.5 m) of contrasting print or solid for strips to make diamond shapes 5⁷/₈ yds (5.4 m) of fabric for backing ³/₄ yd (69 cm) of fabric for binding
You will also need	73" x 73" (185 cm x 185 cm) piece of batting 16¹/₂" or larger square acrylic ruler	73" x 105" (185 cm x 267 cm) piece of batting 16¹/₂" or larger square acrylic ruler
Cut pieces	64 **squares** 9¹/₂" x 9¹/₂" 16 **strips** 25" x 2¹/₂" 8 **binding strips** 2¹/₂" wide	96 **squares** 9¹/₂" x 9¹/₂" 24 **strips** 25" x 2¹/₂" 9 **binding strips** 2¹/₂" wide

memory lane TRADITIONAL

As you can see, color placement can really change the look of this pattern. In this lap quilt version, Gudrun used print fabrics from four color families and planned her block assembly and block placement so that the same colors were grouped together. The black diamonds make the light-to-medium colors sparkle in this lap-size quilt.

Finished Lap Quilt Size: 65" x 65" (165 cm x 165 cm)
Finished Block Size: 16" x 16" (41 cm x 41 cm)

Pieced by Gudrun Erla • Quilted by Harriet Bollig

The smaller traditional version of Memory Lane is constructed in the same manner as the traditional version, but with bright prints and black strips. To make quilt shown, you will need the following.

64 layer cake squares of assorted prints (24 blue, 16 pink, 16 green, and 8 white) ($^3/_8$ yd [30 cm] *each* of 16 assorted prints [6 blue, 4 pink, 4 green, and 2 white] may be used instead, but will provide less variety)

Refer to chart, page 40, for additional fabric requirements.

1. Make each Four Patch using one color of assorted prints. Make 6 blue, 4 pink, 4 green, and 2 white Four Patches.
2. Make the following Unit 3's: 6 blue/pink, 6 blue/green, 2 white/pink, and 2 white/green.
3. When trimming blocks, make sure 16$^1/_2$" edges or marks of ruler are aligned with green or pink fabric side of strip.

This design looks lovely in deep hues. In this version, Block A includes a Nine-Patch center, which adds emphasis to the diagonal lines of the quilt. The second version on page 50 shows just how well this design also works with a brighter, lighter palette.

Finished Twin/Full Quilt Size
73½" x 93⅜" (187 cm x 237 cm)
Finished Block Size
12" x 12" (30 cm x 30 cm)

Pieced by Yvonne Gesk
Quilted by Rita Kroenin

snapshots TRADITIONAL

FABRIC REQUIREMENTS

Yardage is based on 43"/44" (109 cm/112 cm) wide fabric with a "usable" width of 40" (102 cm).
Note: *Fat quarters must be at least 21" x 18" (53 cm x 46 cm).*

- 5 assorted print fat quarters (one *each* of brown, green, purple, red, and gold)
- 1¾ yds (1.6 m) of tan small print
- ⅞ yd (80 cm) of tan large print
- ¼ yd (23 cm) of gold print for Nine Patches
- ⅜ yd (34 cm) *each* of red print #1 and green print #1 for Nine Patches
- ¾ yd (69 cm) *each* of red print #2 and green print #2
- ⅞ yd (80 cm) of brown print
- 2 yds (1.8 m) of fabric for outer border
- 6¾ yds (6.2 m) of fabric for backing*
- ⅞ yd (80 cm) of fabric for binding

You will also need:
- 81" x 101" (206 cm x 257 cm) piece of batting

*Yardage is based on three 81" lengths of fabric. If usable width of fabric (excluding selvages) is 41" or more, two 101" lengths or 5⅝ yds (5.1 m) will be adequate.

CUTTING THE PIECES

Follow **Rotary Cutting**, page 53. Cut strips from yardage from the selvage-to-selvage width of the fabric. Cut strips from fat quarters parallel to long edge. Measurements include 1/4" seam allowances.

From *each* assorted print fat quarter:
- Cut 3 strips 5 1/4" wide. From these strips, cut 12 squares 5 1/4" x 5 1/4". Cut squares *twice* diagonally to make 48 **small triangles**. (You will have a total of 240 triangles.)

From tan small print:
- Cut 16 strips 2 1/2" wide. From these strips, cut 48 **sashings** 2 1/2" x 12 1/2".
- Cut 10 strips 1 1/2" wide. From these strips, cut 24 **small rectangles** 1 1/2" x 8 1/2" and 24 **very small rectangles** 1 1/2" x 6 1/2".

From tan large print:
- Cut 2 strips 8 1/2" wide. From these strips, cut 6 **Block B center squares** 8 1/2" x 8 1/2".
- Cut 1 strip 9 3/4" wide. From this strip, cut 3 squares 9 3/4" x 9 3/4". Cut these squares *twice* diagonally to make 12 **large triangles**. (You will use 10 and have 2 left over.)
- Cut 2 squares 3 3/4" x 3 3/4". Cut these squares *once* diagonally to make 4 **medium triangles**.

From gold print:
- Cut 3 strips 2 1/2" wide. From these strips, cut 48 **small squares** 2 1/2" x 2 1/2".

From *each* of red print #1 and green print #1:
- Cut 1 strip 3 3/8" wide. From this strip, cut 6 **large squares** 3 3/8" x 3 3/8".
- Cut 2 strips 3" wide. From these strips, cut 24 **medium square A's** 3" x 3".

From *each* of red print #2 and green print #2:
- Cut 2 strips 3" wide. From these strips, cut 17 **medium square B's** 3" x 3".
- Cut 6 strips 2 1/2" wide. From these strips, cut 12 **large rectangles** 2 1/2" x 10" and 12 **medium rectangles** 2 1/2" x 8 1/2".

From brown print:
- Cut 8 **inner border strips** 2 1/2" wide.
- Cut 2 strips 2 1/2" wide. From these strips, cut 17 **sashing squares** 2 1/2" x 2 1/2".

From fabric for outer border:
- Cut 10 **outer border strips** 6 1/2" wide.

From fabric for binding:
- Cut 10 **binding strips** 2 1/2" wide.

MAKING THE BLOCK A'S

Follow **Piecing**, page 54, and **Pressing**, page 55, to make quilt top. Use 1/4" seam allowances throughout. Measurements provided include seam allowances.

1. Draw a diagonal line (corner to corner) on wrong side of *each* red print #1 **large square** and red print #1 **medium square A**.
2. Matching right sides, place 1 red print #1 **medium square A** on top of 1 green print #1 **medium square A**. Stitch 1/4" from each side of drawn line *(Fig. 1)*. Cut along drawn line and press seam allowances to darker fabric to make 2 **Triangle-Square A's**. Trim Triangle-Square A's to 2 1/2" x 2 1/2". Make 48 **Triangle-Square A's**.

Fig. 1

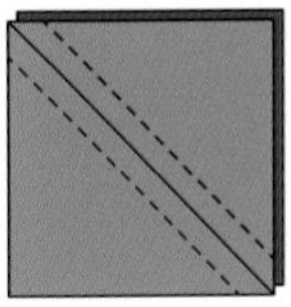

Triangle-Square A
(make 48)

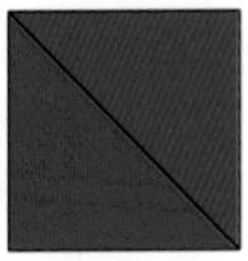

3. Using red print #1 **large squares** and green print #1 **large squares**, make 12 **Triangle-Square B's**. Triangle-Square B should measure 3" x 3".

Triangle-Square B (make 12)

4. Draw a diagonal line (corner to corner and perpendicular to seam) on wrong side of 6 of **Triangle-Square B's**.

5. Matching right sides and seams and with like fabrics opposite, place 1 marked **Triangle-Square B** on top of 1 unmarked **Triangle-Square B**. Stitch ¼" from each side of drawn line *(Fig. 2)*. Cut along drawn line and press seam allowances to one side to make 2 **Hourglasses**. Trim Hourglasses to 2½" x 2½". Make 12 Hourglasses.

Fig. 2

Hourglass (make 12)

6. Sew 2 **Triangle-Square A's** and 1 gold print **small square** together to make **Unit 1**. Make 24 Unit 1's.

Unit 1 (make 24)

7. Sew 2 gold print **small squares** and 1 **Hourglass** together to make **Unit 2**. Make 12 Unit 2's.

Unit 2 (make 12)

8. Sew 2 **Unit 1's** and 1 **Unit 2** together to make **Nine Patch**. Nine Patch should measure 6½" x 6½". Make 12 Nine Patches.

Nine Patch (make 12)

9. Sew 2 tan small print **very small rectangles** and 1 **Nine Patch** together to make **Unit 3**. Make 12 Unit 3's.

Unit 3 (make 12)

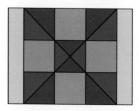

10. Sew 2 tan small print **small rectangles** and 1 **Unit 3** together to make **Unit 4**. Make 12 Unit 4's.

Unit 4 (make 12)

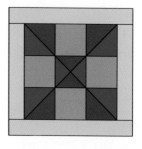

11. Sew 2 small assorted print **small triangles** together to make **Unit 5**. Make 48 Unit 5's.

Unit 5 (make 48)

12. Sew 3 small assorted print **small triangles** together to make **Unit 6**. Make 48 Unit 6's.

Unit 6 (make 48)

Sew 4 **Unit 6's** and 1 **Unit 4** together to make **Unit 7**. Make 12 Unit 7's.

Unit 7 (make 12)

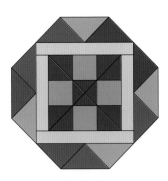

Sew 4 **Unit 5's** and 1 **Unit 7** together to make **Block A**. Block A should measure 12^1/$_2$" x 12^1/$_2$". Make 12 Block A's.

Block A (make 12)

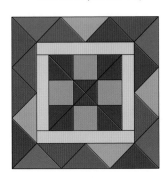

MAKING THE BLOCK B'S

In same manner as previous, use red print #2 **medium square B's** and green print #2 **medium square B's** to make 34 **Triangle-Square C's**. Trim Triangle-Square C's to 2^1/$_2$" x 2^1/$_2$".

Triangle-Square C (make 34)

Sew 2 **Triangle-Square C's** and 1 red print #2 **medium rectangle** together to make **Unit 8**. Make 12 Unit 8's.

Unit 8 (make 12)

3. Sew 2 green print #2 **medium rectangles** and 1 tan large print **Block B center square** together to make **Unit 9**. Make 6 Unit 9's.

Unit 9 (make 6)

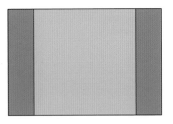

4. Sew 2 **Unit 8's** and 1 **Unit 9** together to make **Block B**. Block B should measure 12^1/$_2$" x 12^1/$_2$". Make 6 Block B's.

Block B (make 6)

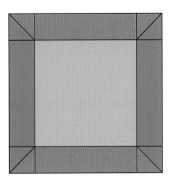

MAKING THE SIDE AND CORNER UNITS

1. Sew 1 **Triangle-Square C** and 1 green print #2 **large rectangle** together to make **Unit 10**. Make 4 Unit 10's.

Unit 10 (make 4)

2. Sew 1 red print #2 **large rectangle** and 1 tan large print **large triangle** together to make **Unit 11**. Make 4 Unit 11's.

Unit 11 (make 4)

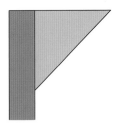

3. Sew 1 **Unit 10** and 1 **Unit 11** together. Trim rectangles even with triangle *(Fig. 3)* to make **Side Unit A**. Make 4 Side Unit A's.

Fig. 3   **Side Unit A** (make 4)

4. Sew 1 **Triangle-Square C** and 1 red print #2 **large rectangle** together to make **Unit 12**. Make 6 Unit 12's.

Unit 12 (make 6)

5. Sew 1 green print #2 **large rectangle** and 1 tan large print **large triangle** together to make **Unit 13**. Make 6 Unit 13's.

Unit 13 (make 6)

6. Sew 1 **Unit 12** and 1 **Unit 13** together. In same manner as previous, trim rectangles even with triangle to make **Side Unit B**. Make 6 Side Unit B's.

Side Unit B (make 6)

7. Sew 1 red print #2 **large rectangle** and 1 tan large print **medium triangle** together. Trim rectangle even with triangle *(Fig. 4)* to make **Corner Unit A**. Make 2 Corner Unit A's.

Fig. 4   **Corner Unit A** (make 2)

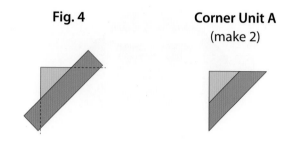

8. Sew 1 green print #2 **large rectangle** and 1 tan large print **medium triangle** together. In same manner as previous, trim rectangle even with triangle to make **Corner Unit B**. Make 2 Corner Unit B's.

Corner Unit B (make 2)

ASSEMBLING THE QUILT TOP CENTER

*Refer to **Assembly Diagram**, page 49, for placement. Pay special attention to placement of red and green rectangles in Block B's, Side Units, and Corner Units.*

1. Arrange Blocks, Side Units, sashings, and sashing squares into diagonal **Rows**.
2. Sew diagonal **Rows** together. Sew sashings and Corner Unit A's to top left and bottom right, and Corner Unit B's to top right and bottom left to complete quilt top center. Trim outer edges as needed.

ADDING THE BORDERS

1. Using diagonal seams, sew **inner border strips** together to make one continuous strip *(Fig. 5)*.

Fig. 5

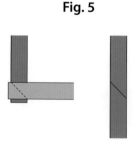

Assembly Diagram

Corner Unit A
Sashing
Row A
Sashing Row A
Row B
Sashing Row B
Row C
Corner Unit B
Side Unit A
Sashing Row C
Side Unit B
Row D
Sashing Row D
Row E
Sashing Row E
Side Unit B
Row F
Sashing
Side Unit A
Corner Unit B
Corner Unit A

Measure *length* across center of quilt top center. Cut 2 **side inner borders** from continuous strip. Matching centers and corners, sew side inner borders to quilt top center.

Measure *width* across center of quilt top center (including added borders). Cut 2 **top/bottom inner borders** from continuous strip. Matching centers and corners, sew top/bottom borders to quilt top center.

In the same manner, use **outer border strips** to add **top/bottom** and **side outer borders** to quilt top.

COMPLETING THE QUILT

1. Follow **Machine Quilting**, page 55, to mark, layer, and quilt as desired. Quilt shown was machine quilted. The sashings and inner border were quilted in the ditch. A curvy motif was quilted in each Block A and in the center of each Block B. A leaf pattern was quilted in the sashings. The side units, corner units, outer border, and the outer portions of Block B's were meander quilted.

2. Follow **Making a Hanging Sleeve**, page 57, if a hanging sleeve is desired.

3. Use **binding strips** and follow **Binding**, page 57, to bind quilt.

For this version of Snapshots, Gudrun replaced the Nine-Patch centers of Block A's with a single fabric square. Visually, this opens up the look of the quilt and gives its style a more casual feel.

Finished Twin/Full Quilt Size: $73^1/_2$" x $93^3/_8$" (187 cm x 237 cm)
Finished Block Size: 12" x 12" (30 cm x 30 cm)

Pieced by Gudrun Erla • Quilted by Randi Helling

The modern version of Snapshots is constructed the same a the traditional version with these exceptions.

1. Bright and graphic prints were used along with whit print for the sashings.
2. The Nine Patches in Block A's are replaced with $6^1/_2$" x $6^1/_2$" squares (cut size) which are cut from the same fabric as the centers of Block B's. This will requi an additional $1/_2$ yd (46 cm) of fabric. You will not nee the fabric for the Nine Patches.

SNAPSHOTS OPTIONAL SIZES

	CRIB	LAP
Finished size	53³/₄" x 73⁵/₈" (137 cm x 187 cm)	73⁵/₈" x 73⁵/₈" (187 cm x 187 cm)
Blocks	6 Block A's and 2 Block B's	9 Block A's and 4 Block B's

Fabric requirements	5 fat quarters of assorted prints (1 *each* of brown, green, purple, red, and gold)
	⁷/₈ yd (80 cm) of tan small print
	⁵/₈ yd (57 cm) (traditional)
	  or ⁷/₈ yd (80 cm) (modern) of tan large print
	¹/₄ yd (23 cm) of gold print (traditional)
	¹/₄ yd (23 cm) *each* of red print #1 and green print #1 (traditional)
	³/₈ yd (34 cm) *each* of red print #2 and green print #2
	⁵/₈ yd (57 cm) of brown print
	1¹/₂ yds (1.4 m) of fabric for outer border
	4⁵/₈ yds (4.2 m) of fabric for backing
	⁵/₈ yd (57 cm) of fabric for binding
		5 fat quarters of assorted prints (1 *each* of brown, green, purple, red, and gold)
		1³/₈ yds (1.3 m) of tan small print
		⁵/₈ yd (57 cm) (traditional)
		  or 1 yd (91 cm) (modern) of tan large print
		¹/₄ yd (23 cm) of gold print (traditional)
		³/₈ yd (34 cm) *each* of red print #1 and green print #1 (traditional)
		¹/₂ yd (46 cm) *each* of red print #2 and green print #2
		⁵/₈ yd (57 cm) of brown print
		1⁷/₈ yds (1.7 m) of fabric for outer border
		6⁷/₈ yds (6.3 m) of fabric for backing
		³/₄ yd (69 cm) of fabric for binding

You will also need	62" x 82" (157 cm x 208 cm) piece of batting	82" x 82" (208 cm x 208 cm) piece of batting
Cut pieces *(Pieces are listed in the same order as in **Cutting the Pieces**, page 45.)*	120 **small triangles** from 30 squares 5¹/₄" x 5¹/₄" cut *twice* diagonally 24 **sashings** 2¹/₂" x 12¹/₂" 12 **small rectangles** 1¹/₂" x 8¹/₂" 12 **very small rectangles** 1¹/₂" x 6¹/₂" 2 **Block B center squares** 8¹/₂" x 8¹/₂" 6 **large triangles** from 2 squares 9³/₄" x 9³/₄" cut *twice* diagonally 4 **medium triangles** from 2 squares 3³/₄" x 3³/₄" cut *once* diagonally 24 **small squares** 2¹/₂" x 2¹/₂"* 6 (3 *each* color) **large squares** 3³/₈" x 3³/₈"* 24 (12 *each* color) **medium square A's** 3" x 3"* 14 (7 *each* color) **medium square B's** 3" x 3" 16 (8 *each* color) **large rectangles** 2¹/₂" x 10" 8 (4 *each* color) **medium rectangles** 2¹/₂" x 8¹/₂" 6 **inner border strips** 2¹/₂" wide 7 **sashing squares** 2¹/₂" x 2¹/₂" 7 **outer border strips** 6¹/₂" wide 7 **binding strips** 2¹/₂" wide *For modern, replace with 6 **Block A center squares** 6¹/₂" x 6¹/₂"	180 **small triangles** from 45 squares 5¹/₄" x 5¹/₄" cut *twice* diagonally 36 **sashings** 2¹/₂" x 12¹/₂" 18 **small rectangles** 1¹/₂" x 8¹/₂" 18 **very small rectangles** 1¹/₂" x 6¹/₂" 4 **Block B center squares** 8¹/₂" x 8¹/₂" 8 **large triangles** from 2 squares 9³/₄" x 9³/₄" cut *twice* diagonally 4 **medium triangles** from 2 squares 3³/₄" x 3³/₄" cut *once* diagonally 36 **small squares** 2¹/₂" x 2¹/₂"* 10 (5 *each* color) **large squares** 3³/₈" x 3³/₈"* 36 (18 *each* color) **medium square A's** 3" x 3"* 24 (12 *each* color) **medium square B's** 3" x 3" 20 (10 *each* color) **large rectangles** 2¹/₂" x 10" 16 (8 *each* color) **medium rectangles** 2¹/₂" x 8¹/₂" 7 **inner border strips** 2¹/₂" wide 12 **sashing squares** 2¹/₂" x 2¹/₂" 9 **outer border strips** 6¹/₂" wide 9 **binding strips** 2¹/₂" wide *For modern, replace with 9 **Block A center squares** 6¹/₂" x 6¹/₂"

SNAPSHOTS OPTIONAL SIZES

	QUEEN	KING
Finished size	$93^3/_8$" x $93^3/_8$" (237 cm x 237 cm)	$113^1/_4$" x $113^1/_4$" (288 cm x 288 cm)
Blocks	16 Block A's and 9 Block B's	25 Block A's and 16 Block B's

Fabric requirements	10 fat quarters of assorted prints (2 *each* of brown, green, purple, red, and gold)
	$2^3/_8$ yds (2.2 m) of tan small print
	$1^1/_8$ yds (1 m) (traditional)
	  or $1^3/_4$ yds (1.6 m) (modern) of tan large print
	$3/_8$ yd (34 cm) of gold print (traditional)
	$1/_2$ yd (46 cm) *each* of red print #1 and green print #1 (traditional)
	$7/_8$ yd (80 cm) *each* of red print #2 and green print #2
	$7/_8$ yd (80 cm) of brown print
	$2^1/_4$ yds (2.1 m) of fabric for outer border
	$8^1/_2$ yds (7.8 m) of fabric for backing
	$7/_8$ yd (80 cm) of fabric for binding
		15 fat quarters of assorted prints (3 *each* of brown, green, purple, red, and gold)
		$3^5/_8$ yd (3.3 m) of tan small print
		$1^3/_8$ yds (1.3 m) (traditional)
		  or $2^3/_8$ yds (2.2 m) (modern) of tan large print
		$5/_8$ yd (57 cm) of gold print (traditional)
		$5/_8$ yd (57 cm) *each* of red print #1 and green print #1 (traditional)
		$1^3/_8$ yds (1.3 m) *each* of red print #2 and green print #2
		$1^1/_8$ yds (1 m) of brown print
		$2^5/_8$ yds (2.4 m) of fabric for outer border
		$13^1/_2$ yds (12.3 m) of fabric for backing
		1 yd (91 cm) of fabric for binding

You will also need	101" x 101" (257 cm x 257 cm) piece of batting	121" x 121" (307 cm x 307 cm) piece of batting
Cut pieces (Pieces are listed in the same order as in **Cutting the Pieces**, page 45.)	320 **small triangles** from 80 squares $5^1/_4$" x $5^1/_4$" cut *twice* diagonally 64 **sashings** $2^1/_2$" x $12^1/_2$" 32 **small rectangles** $1^1/_2$" x $8^1/_2$" 32 **very small rectangles** $1^1/_2$" x $6^1/_2$" 9 **Block B center squares** $8^1/_2$" x $8^1/_2$" 12 **large triangles** from 3 squares $9^3/_4$" x $9^3/_4$" cut *twice* diagonally 4 **medium triangles** from 2 squares $3^3/_4$" x $3^3/_4$" cut *once* diagonally 64 **small squares** $2^1/_2$" x $2^1/_2$"* 16 (8 *each* color) **large squares** $3^3/_8$" x $3^3/_8$"* 64 (32 *each* color) **medium square A's** 3" x 3"* 48 (24 *each* color) **medium square B's** 3" x 3" 28 (14 *each* color) **large rectangles** $2^1/_2$" x 10" 36 (18 *each* color) **medium rectangles** $2^1/_2$" x $8^1/_2$" 9 **inner border strips** $2^1/_2$" wide 24 **sashing squares** $2^1/_2$" x $2^1/_2$" 11 **outer border strips** $6^1/_2$" wide 11 **binding strips** $2^1/_2$" wide *For modern, replace with 16 **Block A center squares** $6^1/_2$" x $6^1/_2$"	500 **small triangles** from 125 squares $5^1/_4$" x $5^1/_4$" cut *twice* diagonally 100 **sashings** $2^1/_2$" x $12^1/_2$" 50 **small rectangles** $1^1/_2$" x $8^1/_2$" 50 **very small rectangles** $1^1/_2$" x $6^1/_2$" 16 **Block B center squares** $8^1/_2$" x $8^1/_2$" 16 **large triangles** from 4 squares $9^3/_4$" x $9^3/_4$" cut *twice* diagonally 4 **medium triangles** from 2 squares $3^3/_4$" x $3^3/_4$" cut *once* diagonally 100 **small squares** $2^1/_2$" x $2^1/_2$"* 26 (13 *each* color) **large squares** $3^3/_8$" x $3^3/_8$"* 100 (50 *each* color) **medium square A's** 3" x 3"* 80 (40 *each* color) **medium square B's** 3" x 3" 36 (18 *each* color) **large rectangles** $2^1/_2$" x 10" 64 (32 *each* color) **medium rectangles** $2^1/_2$" x $8^1/_2$" 11 **inner border strips** $2^1/_2$" wide 40 **sashing squares** $2^1/_2$" x $2^1/_2$" 13 **outer border strips** $6^1/_2$" wide 13 **binding strips** $2^1/_2$" wide *For modern, replace with 25 **Block A center squares** $6^1/_2$" x $6^1/_2$"

o make your quilting easier and more enjoyable,
e encourage you to carefully read all of the general
istructions, study the color photographs, and familiarize
ourself with the individual project instructions before
eginning a project.

ABRICS

ELECTING FABRICS

hoose high-quality, medium-weight 100% cotton
ibrics. All-cotton fabrics hold a crease better, fray less,
nd are easier to quilt than cotton/polyester blends.

ardage requirements listed for each project are based
n 43"/44" wide fabric with a "usable" width of 40" after
hrinkage and trimming selvages. Actual usable width
ill probably vary slightly from fabric to fabric. Our
ecommended yardage lengths should be adequate
or occasional re-squaring of fabric when many cuts are
equired.

While the size of fat quarters may vary slightly, each
hould be at least 21" x 18" (53 x 46 cm). If they are
maller, more fat quarters may be required.

PREPARING FABRICS

using pre-cut fabrics, we do not recommend pre-
ashing. Pre-washing fabrics may cause edges to ravel. As
result, your fat quarters or other pre-cut pieces, may not
e large enough to cut all of the pieces required for your
hosen project.

efore cutting, prepare fabrics with a steam iron set
n cotton and starch or sizing. The starch or sizing will
ive the fabric a crisp finish. This will make cutting more
ccurate and may make piecing easier.

ROTARY CUTTING

*Rotary cutting has brought speed and accuracy to
quiltmaking by allowing quilters to easily cut strips of fabric
and then cut those strips into smaller pieces. It is helpful to
keep pieces separated and identified in zip bags.*

CUTTING FROM YARDAGE

- Place fabric yardage on work surface with fold
  closest to you.

- Cut all strips from the selvage-to-selvage width
  of the fabric unless otherwise indicated in project
  instructions.

- Square left edge of fabric using rotary cutter and
  rulers (*Figs. 1-2*).

Fig. 1

Fig. 2

- To cut each strip required for a project, place ruler over cut edge of fabric, aligning desired marking on ruler with cut edge; make cut *(Fig. 3)*.

Fig. 3

- When cutting several strips from a single piece of fabric, it is important to make sure that cuts remain at a perfect right angle to the fold; square fabric as needed.

CUTTING FROM FAT QUARTERS

- Place fabric flat on work surface with short (18") edge closest to you.

- Square long (21") left edge of fabric in the same manner as for yardage.

- Cut all strips parallel to 21" edge of the fabric unless otherwise indicated in project instructions.

- To cut each strip required for a project, place ruler over left edge of fabric, aligning desired marking on ruler with left edge; make cut.

PIECING

Precise cutting, followed by accurate piecing, will ensure that all pieces of quilt top fit together well.

- Set sewing machine stitch length for approximately 11 stitches per inch.

- Use neutral-colored general-purpose sewing thread (not quilting thread) in needle and in bobbin.

- A consistent $1/4$" seam allowance is *essential*. Presser feet that are $1/4$" are available for most sewing machines.

- When piecing, always place pieces right sides together and match raw edges; pin if necessary.

- Chain piecing saves time and will usually result in more accurate piecing.

- Trim away points of seam allowances that extend beyond edges of sewn pieces.

SEWING STRIPS SET

When there are several strips to assemble into a strip set, first sew strips together into pairs, then sew pairs together to form strip set. To help avoid distortion, sew seams in opposite directions *(Fig. 4)*.

Fig. 4

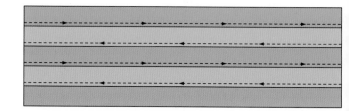

SEWING ACROSS SEAM INTERSECTIONS

When sewing across intersection of two seams, place pieces right sides together and match seams exactly, making sure seam allowances are pressed in opposite directions *(Fig. 5)*.

Fig. 5

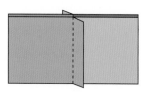

SEWING SHARP POINTS

To ensure sharp points when joining triangular or diagonal pieces, stitch across the center of the "X" (shown in pink) formed on wrong side by previous seams *(Fig. 6)*.

Fig. 6

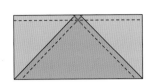

PRESSING

- Use steam iron set on "Cotton" for all pressing.

- Press after sewing each seam.

- To prevent dark fabric seam allowance from showing through light fabric, trim darker seam allowance slightly narrower than lighter seam allowance.

- To press long seams, such as those in long strip sets, without curving or other distortion, lay strips across width of the ironing board.

MACHINE QUILTING

*Quilting holds the three layers (top, batting, and backing) of the quilt together. Because marking, layering, and quilting are interrelated and may be done in different orders depending on circumstances, please read entire **Machine Quilting** section, pages 55-57, before beginning project.*

MARKING QUILTING LINES

Quilting lines may be marked using fabric marking pencils, chalk markers, or water- or air-soluble pens.

Simple quilting designs may be marked with chalk or chalk pencil after basting. A small area may be marked, then quilted, before moving to next area to be marked. Intricate designs should be marked before basting using a more durable marker.

Caution: Pressing may permanently set some marks. **Test** different markers **on scrap fabric** to find one that marks clearly and can be thoroughly removed.

A wide variety of pre-cut quilting stencils, as well as entire books of quilting patterns, are available. Using a stencil makes it easier to mark intricate or repetitive designs.

To make a stencil from a pattern, center template plastic over pattern and use a permanent marker to trace pattern onto plastic. Use a craft knife with single or double blade to cut channels along traced lines *(Fig. 7)*.

Fig. 7

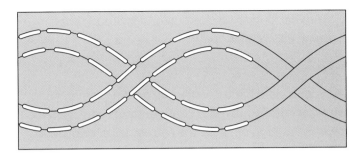

PREPARING THE BACKING

To allow for slight shifting of quilt top during quilting, backing should be approximately 4" larger on all sides. Yardage requirements listed for quilt backings are calculated for 43"/44" wide fabric. Using 90" wide or 108" wide fabric for the backing of a bed-sized quilt may eliminate piecing. To piece a backing using 43"/44" wide fabric, use the following instructions.

1. Measure length and width of quilt top; add 8" to each measurement.

2. **If determined width is 79" or less**, cut backing fabric into two lengths slightly longer than determined *length* measurement. Trim selvages. Place lengths with right sides facing and sew long edges together, forming tube *(Fig. 8)*. Match seams and press along one fold *(Fig. 9)*. Cut along pressed fold to form single piece *(Fig. 10)*.

Fig. 8	**Fig. 9**	**Fig. 10**

3. **If determined width is more than 79"**, it may require less fabric yardage if the backing is pieced horizontally. Divide determined *length* measurement by 40" to determine how many widths will be needed. Cut required number of widths the determined *width* measurement. Trim selvages. Sew long edges together to form single piece.
4. Trim backing to size determined in Step 1; press seam allowances open.

CHOOSING THE BATTING

The appropriate batting will make quilting easier. All cotton or cotton/polyester blend battings work well for machine quilting because the cotton helps "grip" quilt layers."

Types of batting include cotton, polyester, wool, cotton/polyester blend, cotton/wool blend, and silk.

When selecting batting, refer to package labels for characteristics and care instructions. Cut batting same size as prepared backing.

ASSEMBLING THE QUILT

1. Examine wrong side of quilt top closely; trim any seam allowances and clip any threads that may show through front of the quilt. Press quilt top, being careful not to "set" any marked quilting lines.
2. Place backing *wrong* side up on flat surface. Use masking tape to tape edges of backing to surface. Place batting on top of backing fabric. Smooth batting gently, being careful not to stretch or tear. Center quilt top *right* side up on batting.
3. Use 1" rustproof safety pins to "pin-baste" all layers together, spacing pins approximately 4" apart. Begin at center and work toward outer edges to secure all layers. If possible, place pins away from areas that will be quilted, although pins may be removed as needed when quilting.

QUILTING METHODS

Use general-purpose thread in bobbin. Do not use quilting thread. Thread the needle of machine with general-purpose thread or transparent monofilament thread to make quilting blend with quilt top fabrics. Use decorative thread, such as a metallic or contrasting-color general-purpose thread, to make quilting lines stand out more.

Straight-Line Quilting

The term "straight-line" is somewhat deceptive, since curves (especially gentle ones) as well as straight lines can be stitched with this technique.

1. Set stitch length for six to ten stitches per inch and attach walking foot to sewing machine.
2. Determine which section of quilt will have longest continuous quilting line, oftentimes area from center top to center bottom. Roll up and secure each edge of quilt to help reduce the bulk, keeping fabrics smooth. Smaller projects may not need to be rolled.
3. Begin stitching on longest quilting line, using very short stitches for the first $1/4$" to "lock" quilting. Stitch across project, using one hand on each side of walking foot to slightly spread fabric and to guide fabric through machine. Lock stitches at end of quilting line.
4. Continue machine quilting, stitching longer quilting lines first to stabilize quilt before moving on to other areas.

Free-Motion Quilting

Free-motion quilting may be free form or may follow a marked pattern.

1. Attach darning foot to sewing machine and lower or cover feed dogs.
2. Position quilt under darning foot; lower foot. Holding top thread, take a stitch and pull bobbin thread to top of quilt. To "lock" beginning of quilting line, hold top and bobbin threads while making three to five stitches in place.

3. Use one hand on each side of darning foot to slightly spread fabric and to move fabric through the machine. Even stitch length is achieved by using smooth, flowing hand motion and steady machine speed. Slow machine speed and fast hand movement will create long stitches. Fast machine speed and slow hand movement will create short stitches. Move quilt sideways, back and forth, in a circular motion, or in a random motion to create desired designs; do not rotate quilt. Lock stitches at end of each quilting line.

MAKING A HANGING SLEEVE

Attaching a hanging sleeve to the back of a wall hanging or quilt before the binding is added allows your project to be displayed on a wall.

1. Measure width of quilt top edge and subtract 1". Cut piece of fabric 7" wide by determined measurement.
2. Press short edges of fabric piece $1/4$" to wrong side; press edges $1/4$" to wrong side again and machine stitch in place.
3. Matching wrong sides, fold piece in half lengthwise to form tube.
4. Follow project instructions to sew binding to quilt top and to trim backing and batting. Before Blindstitching binding to backing, match raw edges and stitch hanging sleeve to center top edge on back of quilt.
5. Finish binding quilt, treating hanging sleeve as part of backing.
6. Blindstitch bottom of hanging sleeve to backing, taking care not to stitch through to front of quilt.
7. Insert dowel or slat into hanging sleeve.

BINDING

1. Matching short end and using a diagonal seam, sew binding strips called for in project together (*Fig. 11*).

Fig. 11

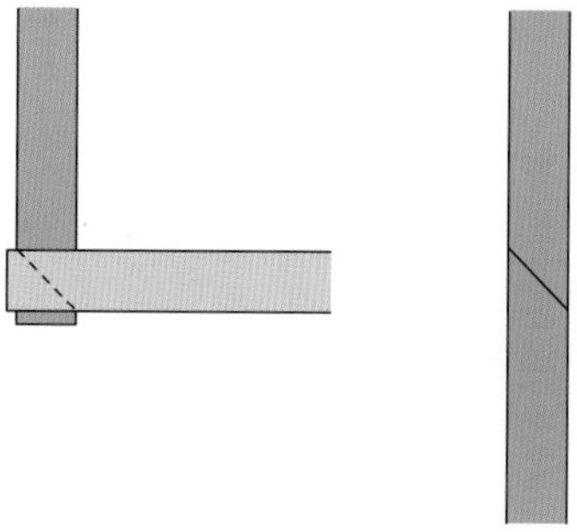

2. Matching wrong sides and raw edges, press strips in half lengthwise.
3. Beginning with one end near center on bottom edge of quilt, lay binding around quilt to make sure that seams in binding will not end up at a corner. Adjust placement if necessary. Matching raw edges of binding to raw edge of quilt top, pin binding to right side of quilt along one edge.
4. When you reach first corner, mark $1/4$" from corner of quilt top (*Fig. 12*).

Fig. 12

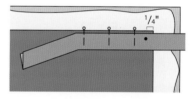

5. Beginning approximately 10" from end of binding and using $1/4$" seam allowance, sew binding to quilt, backstitching at beginning of stitching and at mark (*Fig. 13*). Lift needle out of fabric and clip thread.

Fig. 13

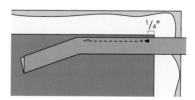

6. Fold binding as shown in **Figs. 14-15** and pin binding to adjacent side, matching raw edges. When you've reached the next corner, mark $1/4$" from edge of quilt top.

Fig. 14   **Fig. 15**

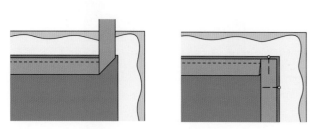

7. Backstitching at edge of quilt top, sew pinned binding to quilt *(Fig. 16)*; backstitch at the next mark. Lift needle out of fabric and clip thread.

Fig. 16

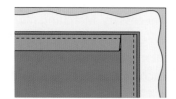

8. Continue sewing binding to quilt, stopping approximately 10" from starting point *(Fig. 17)*.

Fig. 17

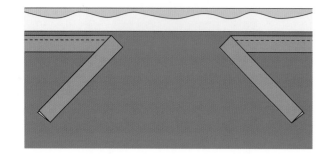

9. Bring beginning and end of binding to center of opening and fold each end back, leaving a $1/4$" space between folds *(Fig. 18)*. Finger press folds.

Fig. 18

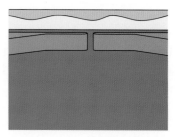

10. Unfold ends of binding and draw a line across wrong side in finger-pressed crease. Draw a line through the lengthwise pressed fold of binding at the same spot to create a cross mark. With edge of ruler at cross mark, line up 45° angle marking on ruler with one long side of binding. Draw a diagonal line from edge to edge. Repeat on remaining end, making sure that the two diagonal lines are angled the same way *(Fig. 19)*.

Fig. 19

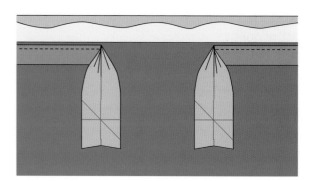

1. Matching right sides and diagonal lines, pin binding ends together at right angles *(Fig. 20)*.

Fig. 20

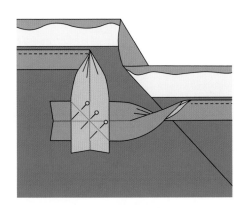

2. Machine stitch along diagonal line *(Fig. 21)*, removing pins as you stitch.

Fig. 21

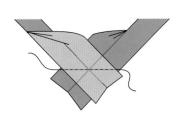

3. Lay binding against quilt to double check that it is correct length.
4. Trim binding ends, leaving ¹/₄" seam allowance; press seam allowances open. Stitch binding to quilt.
5. Trim backing and batting a scant ¹/₄" larger than quilt top so that batting and backing will fill the binding when it is folded over to quilt backing.

16. On one edge of quilt, fold binding over to quilt backing and pin pressed edge in place, covering stitching line *(Fig. 22)*. On adjacent side, fold binding over, forming a mitered corner *(Fig. 23)*. Repeat to pin remainder of binding in place.

Fig. 22   **Fig. 23**

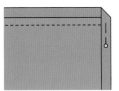 

17. Blindstitch *(Fig. 24)* binding to backing, taking care not to stitch through to front of quilt.

Fig. 24

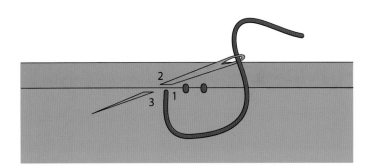

Metric Conversion Chart

Inches x 2.54 = centimeters (cm)   Yards x .9144 = meters (m)
Inches x 25.4 = millimeters (mm)   Yards x 91.44 = centimeters (cm)
Inches x .0254 = meters (m)   Centimeters x .3937 = inches (")
                                   Meters x 1.0936 = yards (yd)

Standard Equivalents

1/8"	3.2 mm	0.32 cm	1/8 yard	11.43 cm	0.11 m
1/4"	6.35 mm	0.635 cm	1/4 yard	22.86 cm	0.23 m
3/8"	9.5 mm	0.95 cm	3/8 yard	34.29 cm	0.34 m
1/2"	12.7 mm	1.27 cm	1/2 yard	45.72 cm	0.46 m
5/8"	15.9 mm	1.59 cm	5/8 yard	57.15 cm	0.57 m
3/4"	19.1 mm	1.91 cm	3/4 yard	68.58 cm	0.69 m
7/8"	22.2 mm	2.22 cm	7/8 yard	80 cm	0.8 m
1"	25.4 mm	2.54 cm	1 yard	91.44 cm	0.91 m